A Tale of Two Kitties
presents

VOLUME THREE

WHAT HAPPENS WHEN WE DIE?

Written by Julie Hasling

Photo-illustrated by Lynn Hasling Pellerin

Order this book online at www.trafford.com
or email orders@trafford.com

Most Trafford titles are also available at major online book retailers.

 **www.trafford.com**

North America & international
toll-free: 844 688 6899 (USA & Canada)
fax: 812 355 4082

Our mission is to efficiently provide the world's finest, most comprehensive book publishing service, enabling every author to experience success. To find out how to publish your book, your way, and have it available worldwide, visit us online at www.trafford.com

Because of the dynamic nature of the Internet, any web addresses or links contained in this book may have changed since publication and may no longer be valid. The views expressed in this work are solely those of the author and do not necessarily reflect the views of the publisher, and the publisher hereby disclaims any responsibility for them.

ISBN: 978-1-4269-6847-1

Library of Congress Control Number: 2011907151

Print information available on the last page.

Trafford rev. 01/03/2024

THIS BOOK BELONGS TO

_____

FROM

_____

DEDICATION

This book, along with volume one and two of the series, is dedicated to my Savior, Lord and King Jesus Christ. The books were given to me through the inspiration of the Holy Spirit. Jesus is the true author of the writings – I am merely the transcriber.

Julie Hasling

12, **WHEN ADAM SINNED,** sin entered the entire human race. Adam's sin brought death, so death spread to everyone, for everyone sinned.

18, **YES, ADAM'S ONE SIN** brought condemnation upon everyone, but Christ's one act of righteousness makes all people right in God's sight and gives them life.

19, **BECAUSE ONE PERSON** disobeyed God, many people became sinners. But because one other person obeyed God, many people will be made right in God's sight.

ROMANS 5:12, 18 & 19 (NLT)

Chico woke up one morning
and was ever so sad,
for he thought of the friend
that he once had.

Chico's heart grew heavy
with such sorrow and grief,
and he paced through the
house in search of relief.

Bogart woke from his slumber ever so groggy,
his eyes were glazed over and his thoughts were
still foggy.

But he knew little Chico was greatly in need, so he
thought, "What a great time to do a good deed!"

Bogart shook his head twice and tried to awaken,
just to let Chico know he would not be forsaken.

He jump off his perch
which was very close by,
placed his paw around
Chico and helped
him to cry.

Chico cried, "Ole'
Sam died when I
was still young,
from an illness that
lodged way deep in
his lung...."

Yes, he had a grave illness which took him away, now I become sad when I think of him today.

Bogart, why do we die? What happens next? I really want to know but it seems so complex."

Bogart took a deep breath and opened his mouth, to explain the whole story of what life was about.

He said....

"The story begins way back in a garden, when God formed man and named him Adam. God then made a woman whose name was Eve. He married them both, and they vowed never to leave. God gave a command that they should not eat, from a tree in that garden which fruit was so sweet."

"God told both of them if
they ate it they'd die, and God spoke
the truth because He never would lie.
Now the serpent was tricky, who lived in the land,
and he came to the woman to question God's
command. He asked, 'Did God really say you couldn't
eat of this tree? You won't die,' hissed the serpent, 'just
eat and you'll see!' The woman reached out and then
took a bite; she gave some to Adam but it was not right."

"For they disobeyed God
and sin entered their heart,
and it tore both of them
completely apart.

Their eyes were then opened
and they felt so much shame,
for what they had done
yet each other they blamed.

They were torn from
God's presence
that very same day,
and could no longer visit
with Him the same way.

Their sin was so serious;
this is the reason why,
now their bodies would
grow old and
eventually die.

Then God cursed the serpent who told the great lie,
who tricked them to eat and caused them to die."

Bogart said, "Now everything dies because of Adam's sin, and we also will die because we are his kin." He said, "Everything's here for a purpose and reason, and everything lives for a time and a season. But the birds and the trees will eventually die, and the insects and frogs return where they lie. Your body will die, because of the sin, but you will live on, if you have Jesus within. Now this is important I really must say, in getting to heaven, there's only one way."

"You must ask Jesus to be your Lord and your Savior,
for you can't enter in just on good behavior.
You must ask forgiveness and repent of your sin,
and invite Jesus Christ to live forever within.
He died for your sins; a great price
to pay, so you could be saved and
live forever one day."

Chico thought for a moment
on the things Bogart said,
then he closed his
teary eyes and lowered
his head.

Bogart showed little Chico
just how he should pray,
Chico turned from his sin
and was forgiven that day.

Chico felt so much
better now that
he saw things anew;
one day he'd see
Sam, the friend
he once knew.

Bogart washed Chico's face and the tears from his cheek,
and gave him a hug as he continued to speak.

Bogart told him what happened to the old cat next door.
It was Raggs whom Chico had never met before.

He said, "There's this old guy who lives right next door, and he's ever so sad and won't talk anymore.

He won't eat anything and he rarely will sleep. He just stares out the window and continues to weep.

He lost his close friend just a few weeks ago, now he's stricken with grief and is feeling quite low. He's all alone now; he has no one at all, Why don't you visit or give him a call?"

Chico said, "But I really don't know just what I should say..." though deep in his heart he wanted to obey.

Then Bogart gave Chico a few good suggestions, for his puzzling mind and all of his questions.

He said, "You can be a good friend to someone in need. You could sit or just listen or do a good deed. You could be very quiet or have some small talk; you could take him some food
or go for a walk."

Chico's eyes lit up bright and he knew what to do. He rushed to his toy box that was red and bright blue.

He search through and through then found his best toy, saying, "I'll give it to Raggs for him to enjoy!"

Chico strutted across the lawn with the toy in his jaws, then sat at the door and for a moment he paused.

He knocked on the door, but ever so slight, then he sat very still and was ever polite.

There was silence inside, no response right away, but Chico persisted and thought he should stay.

Raggs peered through the crack of his tattered front door, and Chico quivered a moment then shook to the core.

When the door slowly opened, Chico saw his sad face. They greeted each other and walked in the place. Chico told him what life and death were about, and with Jesus, he'd see his dear friend without doubt.

Then they spoke a bit longer and cried a time or two, and when they were finished they were no longer blue.

Chico found something special he had not known before, a friendship with Raggs who lived right next door! Though they both lost a friend which could not be replaced, they did find each other as they sat and embraced.

Chico ran home to Bogart and told him the way he had gained more than just a new friend that day.

"We may feel such great sorrow when we lose a good friend, but in time," Chico said, "your heart will surely mend. In the meantime there's something that we all can do. We can comfort our friends in the things they go through."

Chico still visits Raggs at least once a week.
They sit and watch birds or simply stroll down
the creek.

They talk about things and the fun they once had.
They sit very close and are ever so glad.

The friendship they have is ever so rare, for it was
born out of grief and the things that they share.

THE END

PRAYER OF SALVATION

Dear Jesus,
I admit that I am a
sinner and have not
always done what is
right. I believe You
died on the cross for
me and rose again
so that I could live
forever with You
in Heaven one day.
I accept Your gift of
eternal life today.
Jesus, please forgive
me and come into my
heart right now.
Amen.

What Happens When We Die? is the third in a series of Christ-centered children's books that feature two cats, Chico and Bogart, as they explore biblical principles and issues in life. This book has been written in an effort to explain, in simple terms, what happens to us upon the death of the body.

After a person dies, he/she is escorted to either Heaven or Hell depending on which place they have chosen to live. Yes, the place where we will dwell eternally is our CHOICE and not a feeling or a wish, chance or luck of the draw. We can either choose to accept Jesus' free gift of salvation and live forever with Him or reject it and spend eternity separated from Him in Hell.

Eternal life is not something we can earn through good deeds or by being a good person, it is a gift from God that is received through confession, repentance from sin and believing on Jesus.

God saved you by his special favor when you believed. And you can't take credit for this; it is a gift from God. Salvation is not a reward for the good things we have done so none of us can boast about it. Ephesians 2:8-9a (NLT)

We now have a choice to make – we can either accept Jesus's sacrificial death as payment for our sins and live with Him forever or reject this free gift and choose to spend eternity in Hell. It is simply our choice.

The model prayer in this book is a guide to help children open their hearts and accept God's free gift of eternal life.

Won't you accept God's free gift today?

About the Author...

Julie Hasling lives in Tomball, Texas, with her husband, Alan, along with her two cats, Bogart and Chico. Julie, an ordained minister, and her husband serve as elders at Willowbrook Church in Houston, Texas.

A Tale of Two Kitties series was birthed from Julie's passion for God and her love for her cats. Much of her material has been inspired simply by watching her cats do what they do best – entertain!

After living with and observing her cats for nearly two decades she has become well accustomed to each of their specific personalities, habits and antics. Julie has attempted to capture her cat's individualities, along with Scripture and events from her own life and incorporate them into life lessons that children can understand and apply.

Printed in the United States
by Baker & Taylor Publisher Services